Dear Africa

Epistles from your sun

Ruxton Mudhabuko

Edited by Justice E. T. Mukuchura

DEDICATION

I dedicate this book to my father, Mr. Furguson Mudhabuko and late mother, Mrs. Rosemary Marango-Mudhabuko, thank you for bringing me forth. To the Mudhabuko siblings; Dakarai, Bernadette, Garikai and not forgetting my dearest and nearest Melany Makarange, I salute you all.

CONTENTS

ACKNOWLEDGMENTS

This publication could not have been possible without the inspiration from Mr. Furguson Mudhabuko who planted this seed, and Andrews Tekkekara (S.J.) with Peter Rugora whose teachings enlightened me. Special thanks to you guys. I would also like to say I am indebted to Mr. Justice E. T. Mukuchura, for his patience and contributions to this book, including editing and publishing, you were more than a friend mate.

Elsewhere in the text we have borrowed ideas from our predecessor writers. Where we have quoted, we have made effort to acknowledge the source of the citations. Where we might have overlooked such acknowledgements, we regret such omissions and are ready to make amends once alerted.

PREFACE

Before slavery and colonialism visited the African continent, Africa was one big state. It had neither borders nor partitions, but one big nation. Africans lived as one big family. For them everything was engrossed in nature. They were not much of a plastic society that is not in touch with the rhythm of nature. They identified themselves with nature and became one with and from it. The tree depended on people and they also depended on it. Even the grass, soil and animals, the mountains and valleys too. There was no separation with and from mother nature. Nothing was apart from, but everything was part of it. Life was live and worth living. The African mothers and fathers kindled a fire of brotherhood and oneness to their sons and daughters. Laughter and cheer were the essence. Living together made life easy.

However, the intrusion of other languages, cultures, dispensations, thought matrices, relations and relationships, underestimated the African mind, not withstanding equality of situations and equable conditions. The intruders to

1

obtaining conditions chose to sideline, ignore and even suppress the African situation. Many Africans were taken to Europe to slave in the cane fields and some were strung in the loom and ginning factories. Those who were left in Africa were not spared a tale to tell. They had, on their part, to undergo brutal colonialism and were discriminated against. They had also, like their black brethren and sistren in Europe, been subjected to a form of slavery by their colonial masters and were racially segregated. People like Marcus Aurelius Garvey, Lawyer William Du Bois and others fought against slavery and colonialism. In this dilemma, but in solidarity, Africans fought against colonialism within their different colonially bounded countries, beginning with Ghanaian Kwameh Nkrumah. Africans attained independence and had black rule as was their wish.

Yes Africa got it all, got its independence. Songs of praise to the liberation war heroes were composed and sung. All were and are still happy. But how has progress in nation building and quality of life in Africa been significant, that is, from the time independence was attained? Can one stand and describe Africa as a progressive nation comparable to the colonial masters' progress? On one end we would love to ask how was the economy during the colonial time, in order to know how it is progressing today under our home grown African leaders. It is not a question of bringing back the colonial master back to rule Africa but only to measure the growth of the nation. It is our wish, as Africans, to put more attention and effort on those areas which we should progress. What Africa needs to progress is to put in place a new and probably better system. But the process to bring this better system in Africa is met with great resistance from those in authority, hence nothing comes out by way of Hegelian dialecticism, thus a creation of an undesired system which will not give people the hope for better life is

2

the result.

How much then can the governments of Africa improve their countries' conditions? Is it not suspect to believe that Africa has got it all? With this, satisfaction and abundance come to mind, but that stops vision and blurs the look. What is it that can be pointed as abundant in Africa? Other continents like America have more but until now cannot define themselves as having enough. They still want to go further. Their economies are ideal, but they are not yet satisfied. Africa should be proud of what it presently owns but not to be satisfied with its present status and progress. It still has to grow. We love Africa. We still want to work for it and will work for it. The African soil, is the heart of many and all!

What worries most in Africa is that she has attracted attention from other global players because of her deteriorating industry and the low quality of life earned by her peoples. The deteriorating rate of industrialization only translates to people failing to acquire jobs, and countries producing less for export hence earning less in foreign revenue. This will trigger the employer to pay the labourers low wages hence a low standard of living. Workers' grievances are never addressed. This situation is making the leaders of most respective African countries to lose their grip to an extent that will be alarming even to themselves. The leaders have to do more. The core is failing to hold. The threads have loosened. Ends are never meeting!

1 INTRODUCTORY LETTER

Africa is not forsaken, but is a good platoon of humble inhabitants. It lies on a cliff, between low and high land, between windward and the lee. It is walled round by rocks as if an inland island. With its untamed nature, it is a bed where the weeds grow green from its abandoned bases. It is a long-lone broken land where no one rests except the winds that blow restlessly night and day. What you get are groans and moans. Go to some known countries now, you might as well weep. If you may happen to hear laughter, it is from old memories. There people stand, in what they call their country, looking hither and thither, if ever they talk, it is a whisper, fearing to be loud lest they be whipped, why loud? For them to be a people of word and deed, there must be no high land or low land, the cliff has to crumble. Until the strength of the waves of the high tides(people power) humble the waves of tyranny, genocide and tribalism, we may remain with a long road to foot. We should not spoil ourselves with what our own hands spread. We cry Rwanda, we weep Congo. We are inwardly hospitalized in Mali, we brawl in Nigeria and maul each other down South.

The Africa which all wish for is an Africa with people of the warm heart, of the open mind, of the adventurous spirit, a people who care, who heal hurt lives, who comfort the old and destitute, who challenge and up bring the youth and who know no divisions of cultures or class.

This is the opportune time to embark on the enormous task of actualizing the type of Africa that everyone awaits. We long for an Africa that is people oriented, which strives not only for an economic balance but to identify with everyone in an earnest search for personal wellbeing, social justice, inner peace and happiness, as we struggle to live real personal identity. To be credible and authentic, Africa has to seriously address itself to such vital internal issues like quality of leadership, self-discipline among members and quality of life style among all citizens. The essence of Africa then is living together as a family and equitability sharing the goods of this continent and world at large.

We await a better Africa. An Africa that upholds human rights as a basis for a better society. The Universal Declaration of Human Rights in 1945 provides the best occasion for Africans to reflect seriously on the state of human rights within its own boundaries. The UDHR insists on justice and the dignity of all human beings. It mandates a universal return to justice and dignity for all human beings. It mandates a universal return to justice and equality. The absence of these humanitarian qualities robs the continent of its soul. In Africa we have to uphold the dignity and rights of every individual and not the person's status nor the process by which human power is delegated or attained within the social system.

Taking a leaf, the day to day proceedings of great nations are centred on close monitoring and a search for economic growth. This will issue and guarantee a vibrant wealth base. All citizens of any nation have to be greatly involved in the procedures and proceedings. The growth of a nation needs an effective and efficient citizenry. Therefore in these epistles we expose pointers that highlight the space for the citizen in the African continent as a participant in national benefits.

It is noticeable that Africa is in the doldrums of economic growth. Africa has to proceed with caution on its economic roadmap. Industrialization has remained crippled. Sectors that should bring foreign currency in the country, like mining and tourism, have found their ways hijacked and blocked from transforming the economy. In fact, Africa has to believe in herself and that will be enough as a principle of her growth.

More to it, in order to mould and re-mould the African society in different aspects, education has to be the tool. Emphasis on Africa has been and still being given to the importance of education. Samuel Enoch Stumpfin his book **"Socrates to Satre"** commented that "the chief means of continuous graded economic improvement and social rectification lies in utilization of the opportunities of educating the young to modify prevailing types of thought and desire" (**Samuel Enoch Stumpfin: Socrates to Satre. A history of philosophy,4th edition, 1998, McGrawhill Inc NY**)

However in these letters we want to consider all and sundry vis a vis the African condition enlisting Africans to a better cause, working for a better continent, advancing the living status of many. We also avail ourselves to the discussion of issues and matters on education, women et cetera. We do not exonerate anyone from advancing Africanism, be it pro or pan, as everyone is included.

Good wading for and towards the desired African symbiosis, The African Brotherhood.

3 ON EDUCATION

Careful consideration should be given to the paramount importance of education in the life of Africans. The circumstances of our time need educated youths and certain continuing education of adults. Education is to our advantage. It breaks all the cultural barriers and creates a way for a closer relation both within and without our groups and other nations. Education in Africa has to remain a tool with which growth of mental capabilities is focused. It prepares man to think best in the parameters of himself and his activities. What pertains to him is enhanced hence a growth in his faculties.

Without both formal and informal education man loses the points of life. Formal education is gotten from established institutions where an eventual examination is administered in order to assess the performance of the learner. Informal education is gotten from childhood, that is from our families and also as we grow, through associating with our peers and the world at large. "Education is the mechanism by which a society generates the knowledge necessary for its survival and sustenance and transmits this from one generation to another, largely through processes of instructions to the young. It could be informed in the home, at the workplace or in the playground. More usually it is formalized and is conducted in places and contexts specially set apart for the guidance of the young and the edification of older people. The young are trained to acquire knowledge, skills and aptitudes necessary both for preserving and defending the basic institutions and values of society, as well as for adapting these to meet changing circumstances and new challenges," advises Amazrui.(**General history of Africa viii. Africa since 1935, Ali Amazrui (ed), Califonia, 1993 ENESCO**). Africa should find in education the greatest weapon for nation building and social transformation in her search for economic development. This informs authorities in the educational sector to periodically revise and reform the educational system and its curricula to keep in consonance to prevailing situations. Education should employ the best methods at our disposal, taking account of the African situation. The education acquired by the pupil today is the mirror value of the society of tomorrow. Less education means less acquired skills and poor quality of life for the generality of the target populations. Our continuing challenge is the expansion and revitalization of our educational enterprise so that it offers the best product in human capital development. Education is meant to avail us a progressive leap in building stable political, economic and industrial institutions and an advancement in our cultures and a focused renewal of our established traditions. More so, Africans should have an appreciating intellectual breadth and depth to help themselves to consolidate their position on the continent and to correspondingly compete on the global landscape.

Education is the key to a better society. African leaders of the day have the mandate of nurturing the intellectual faculties of all their broad spectrum of people. Education develops the capacity for sound judgment and prepares the student for professional life. Our education in Africa should rise to meet the needs of our present society. People should be encouraged to take up serious studies so they become professionals. The African youth should be moulded in the love for education and to open up to challenging learning processes. Sertillenges, O.P. laments, "How many young people with the pretension to become workers miserably waste their days, and their strength, the vigor of intelligence, their ideal ! Either they do not work ...... or they work badly capriciously, without knowing what they are nor where they want to go nor how to get there" (**O.P. Sertillenges,The intellectual life. The Mercier Press Nertherlands, 1965.)**What is intended through education is for a single mind to contribute something to the community. An individual's mind has nothing to complete unless it is added to the thought of history and the present in a motion towards a greater and more refined future.. Every person's mind has to contribute something to one or more systems in the society thus making our continent nobler and a precious place to be.

.

Education makes all things new through us. Many things which seem to be difficult will be made clearer and easier. In this case those receiving instruction should not take this service for granted, but seriously. A learned person is one who makes oneself from what has been learnt and fashions oneself around it in a spiral and concentric development model. Sertillenges would sternly say "All that teaching does is to provide us with means of mental activity, as medicine can act on an inert organism, no teaching can succeed with a negligent mind."

The mind is on a journey head-ward to attain the truth and to communicate ideas with the environment. It is our belief that at birth the mind is just a blank slate without anything loaded on it, just like a ship on the dock awaiting an assignment. As one grows the mind begins and continues to load more and more information. Thus the mind is a voyager. What is peculiar, at the dock, is that the ship has to be loaded systematically so that it can accommodate more consignments. Loading the ship haphazardly makes it to carry less load than it is made for. And this analogy categorically applies to the mind. We are born as tabula rasas. In our childhood we begin to acquire information from the environment. These early stages of life from one to seven years are formative years. What is acquired here by the child forms his character and whole person. In developmental psychology studies these early years are so important in the intellectual growth of a person hence should be given more importance. It is here where the categories of the mind are formed. It is where external impressions are received and processed. The building of these mind blocks which are basic in the thinking processes are constituted in the early years of one's growth. They have to be orderly, clear and be formal in order that they are sensitized only to what is true and good and discard the opposite. From these mental categories is where we get a better or a crude society.

Education is in a very special way, the concern for Africans. Education helps people to know themselves, to identify all people as human species, to be economically balanced, to be free people and self capacitating. Education makes us to be able to attain the wholeness of life and create for ourselves a life worth living. Education is beneficial because it brings order. Our minds have to be ordered, thus what we produce with our hands, our actions, and what we say will be in order and ordered for the purpose. The book by Sertillenges states well the point that "Look always for what connects this thing with that, what conditions are necessary for this and for that ; Let this coordination, and not scattered fragments fix itself in your memory." An educated person is in a position to help the community to have objectives rather than to live life without any meaning and without any vision. With education, problems of life are solved. He went on to say that when people have put order in their mind and memory, they will be automatically protected from excessive strain, and will notice that two apparently distinct precepts are, in effect, but one. He claims that garbage, being useless input and only a preserve for the chaotic mind, generally finds no room in an organized whole. It must either serve a purpose, and should it fail to do so it had better go! He sums up by saying "There is something ridiculous in the effort made by a thing, as by a person to intrude into an arrangement where it has no place, which it does not complete or serve"

Our aim as Africans is to carry ourselves far and wide in different aspects of life through education. Humanity realises itself through education, be it formal, informal or non-formal. African States should consolidate their hard won independence and their economies through education. Education is a progressively positive agent for social change. The educational system in Africa is therefore called upon to do more. It has to transform the thinking and attitude of people in ways that facilitate the creation of citizens conscious of development. It has to produce productive and dynamic people who achieve national development goals. We are in an era of accumulating knowledge! Education is there to break all the barriers and avails us the knowledge bases and handles to entrances of development. All the bad habits are broken, likewise, negative attitudes. Through knowledge rituals are not an end but a means for some satisfaction. We put to reason our customs thus enjoy only what benefits us in them. Let love of peace, as Africans, enrich us to be humbly congregated in fighting for higher ideals.

Sadly or stubbornly so, the crop of African leaders we seem to have are defiant to the tenets of libertas academica. The curricula they promulgate alienate the end users from the purpose for which they are designed. Most of our countries need industrialization and commercialization but our people are exposed to lukewarm instruction that does not offer freedom of research and invention. Those that have the acumen to wade deeper into fields requiring productive research are usually underfunded and eventually talked out of the country citing lack of resources. Those that remain to graduate within our numerous campuses are railed through an education that is designed to produce more loyal workers than the needed entrepreneurs. They undertake courses designed by the elite to perpetuate the status quo. Most institutions offer an education of patronage crafted by the ruling elite's propaganda machinery. It is more of patronage indoctrination disguised as national educational frameworks. However, this type of curriculum does not turn around the economies of many an African state, neither does it equip citizens with the directions of focused development. Those at the helm ensure that information and knowledge critical to development are specified and preserved for the consumption of their generations. It is common knowledge that withholding the same affirms one's power. Instead of Africa to give its citizens an education for liberation and development, most countries would rather they have just enough to remain subjects! Perhaps an educated citizenry is perceived as a dangerous lot to lead, but leading the blind seems to overburden the leaders as well. We hope an open and autonomous educational framework designed to research and develop solutions for local problems will soon leave the policy primeval soup and be coupled to the need for development education. We propose that the sooner the better.

4 ON SOCIAL RESPONSIBILITY

The government should by all means avoid unsafe conditions by committing itself to work for the nation. Government should improve the social welfare of people. It should lay principles as a base for better life. The standard of living should improve. People should have jobs and earn enough. If the government earnestly works hard towards improving the social life of all the people, then it will avoid a situation where many people have nothing while a few bath in champagne. All the citizens should enjoy the wealth of their country. The wealth generated today should be enjoyed by many, and in perpetuity.

In every society there is need for an advocacy system comprising professional and dedicated workers who are well advanced in social scientific research to alert the community of and give evaluations and solutions to causes of social strife. Professionals are extensively trained people in their specific areas of specialization. It will be easy to work with what they have come up with from their researches and suggest realistic solutions to aspects of social disadvantage. They have to be knowledgeable, diligent and competitive thus enhancing the reputation of their country and eventually attaining set goals. For professionals to excel in their work, it is important to note that a certain degree of dedication is important, not only to be professionals but to be dedicated professionals.

What we long for through social responsibility is to make Africa a better place to live. We are not at rest because so many of our children live outside natural family environments and some are destitute and vulnerable, sheltering in our streets. In some corners of the continent we have somehow turned a blind eye to these children and our ears have since gone deaf to their plight. Our conscience long retired to a past century's mass grave. The plight of these children has not been solved. This is a social complexity. It needs a warm heart to cut through. We cannot cry that we do not have resources to help them. In fact, we have enough. The problem may be that we have become consumerists, egoists and individualistic. The children's rights to survival, humane treatment and care have been threatened because as their basic rights to education, love or parental guidance have not been warranted. A nation's social responsibility programme is judged by its effort towards the vulnerable. Some countries, as we have observed, go to the extent of providing for the jobless, pay for, or subsidise children's health and education. Africa should move towards such a status.

We have the aged, orphans, widowed, handicapped, terminally ill, pregnant mothers and destitute who require social safety nets to ameliorate their plight. This social disadvantage segregates them from being equal citizens at par with their advantaged counterparts. It is sad that while constitutions are well worded to include safety nets to address their plight, no real commitment is placed by leaders to make them feel the care. They are not part of the rest. In effect they are viewed as non-productive beneficiaries of the national cake and should therefore receive handouts as and when they are available, as if they never were. The majority of these citizens are left to the mercy of civil society organizations who solicit for external funding for their projects. Governments seem to renege on this noble and human responsibility. They neglect their very citizens. Where governments have been witnessed to attend to this plight, it was not without a price. They only receive aid after declaring total allegiance to the ruling elite. "Vote for us and we give you what you need" goes the saying, further violating their rights. Africa must care for its own people, it has the resources and should have the commitment.

Another area of social responsibility leaders have to take a serious look at is civil protection. There is need for an informed approach to natural disasters as well as manmade accidents. Leaders must coerce all employers to put in place social responsibility and workspace safety and welfare programmes. Monitoring and evaluation checks for compliance should be done on a periodical basis. Governments should have updated equipment to inform on oncoming disasters like floods, frosts, droughts, cyclones, tremors and earthquakes. They should put in place communication systems to alert citizens in advance to avoid last minute reactions. A proactive disaster preparedness network should be seen to be functional in order to curb loss of life and property. We should desist from relying solely on outside sources as there is a danger of being misinformed. Our experience in Africa has told us that disaster responses were graded according to tribal and regional hegemonies. The sectors of society viewed as less powerful are generally attended to last even if they were the first to be hit. Linked to disaster preparedness is the issue of civil wars and refugees. While regional blocks have in place mechanisms of handling such socio-political mishaps, countries should have their own in place to proactively respond and react before international effort is invited. What we do not encourage as Africans is for the neighbour to sit back and say "It belongs there not here!"That is unafrican in every respect. If the Illuminate has the Babylonian brotherhood, why can't we have the African Brotherhood, given that Earth belongs to us and not the reptilian Martians!

5 ON COMMUNION AND SELF RELIANCE

Communion is solidarity expressed through recognizing and respecting others as persons, and not as objects for means to an end. If we have this communion in our continent, then justice and peace replace any form of exploitation and manipulation of some by others. No unfair treatment but co-operation will prevail. No greed but sharing will guide resource allocation. In Africa we have peoples of different races, colours, sex and skills. Although we are now more stratified in these artificial categories, these differences remain what they are, artificial, and never a barrier to oneness. The fundamental principle of equality is that you treat others as you treat yourself. Unity should be based on our relationships as humans, period. Therefore, a nation that strives to become in communion needs to encourage dialogue with the different nations and cultures in which it is established. We aspire for a participatory framework, one that gets information and contributions from its members. Each person should participate in the building up of our United Kingdom of Africa, the African Brotherhood deep-seated in our traditional roots and routes.

Communion in Africa needs to be expressed in concrete action, like sharing material goods with the needy, co-operating with one another to safeguard the unity of the community and contributing generously to the common good. Our non-solidarity should account for the bare reality of misery and poverty all over in Africa. In this case someone, somewhere, should stand up to be the voice of the voiceless so that the corrupt government and people should not ignore the poor in society and also stop to rationalize the situations of poverty with optimistic promises. The people want realistic political policies. Even to spiritualize in situations of poverty and misery needs to be avoided as it leads to little or no action being taken.

Communion and solidarity are the best solutions to poverty alleviation in society. Different nations within Africa need to adapt to this concept. Africa needs to be one society, with one leader, as it was under Isis and Horus. Divided nations have failed to come up with solutions to growth. We are advised towards a dissolution of nations in order to realise growth. Those countries which conglomerated into one nation are better off in terms of quality of life. Cases in point include, Russia, CIS, USA or Great Britain. Coming up to be one nation in Africa will ensure that there is enough food for the hungry, clothes for the naked, houses for the homeless, energy for the powerless, good roads for the unshod, education for the blanks and better health services for the sick. Africans need to determine their destiny and should have an integrated development roadmap towards progress. Getting united is the only way a continent like Africa will assume its rightful place on this planet, and not remain the underdeveloped begging partner that it is. Becoming one nation means a sense of oneness is aroused among all Africans. The greatest advantage is that all Africans have a common hope, heritage and vision, have one aim, one being and one destiny defined from procreation, despite distortions by the Reptilian Martians and their Babylonian Brotherhood. We have a lot to share among ourselves, apart from historically. More to this, the concept of unhu/ubuntu stands as the basis of our solidarity and communion. We are one people who need a single self-identity and a sense of belonging in a single nation not demarcated into little states which bring nothing to the table at the end of the day. It is the challenge that the Africans need to resolve if they are to break the enslaving dependence on foreign agencies for funds. Such an undertaking to make Africa united requires commitment and sound economic policies coupled with an adoption of the right mix of priorities. There is a natural mystic of change sweeping throughout the globe, one of economic alignment, of industrial rejuvenation, and one of understanding the position of man on the universe and his attitude towards mother nature. We must encourage a democratic approach in interpreting and promulgating economic policies and distributing resources in order to bring about meaningful benefits to our future generations. We are currently enjoying some benefits from the development of information and communication technologies which have turned this earth into one global village, that is home to the entire family of this known world. We have to however journey together as one state of Africa as long as there is sincere openness, commitment, active participation and dialogue amongst ourselves, including our so called leaders. This positive approach will yield not only a strong industrialized entity which will enjoy not only economic boost, but which mostly values the oneness of all its peoples, hence we will unite under the axiom, "United we stand, divided we fall" This is our mission as we endeavour to establish a forceful, powerful State of Africa. This must be inculcated into our peoples' way of life, religion and ultimately in our concrete existence.

Such a task calls for the wholehearted co-operation of all, under the principle of love, discipline and self-commitment.

6 ON AID AFRICA

Africa needs political and economic emancipation! Now the question is whether the world at large, or international organisations will continue to appreciate the challenges faced by Africa. Africa has been marked with the phenomenon of underdevelopment and poverty. It has been downtrodden to a continent of hunger and pain. This is a boggle to humanity's conscience

Underdeveloped countries are essentially countries with a very low standard of living, insufficient progress in well-being and conditions unfavorable for development. Underdeveloped countries have limited capacity to serve, have restricted monetary reserves. Through foreign aid, health systems, education, technology, industrialization and the general quality of life should be expected to improve, else we may not require anything that does not serve! Aid should be designed for the beneficiary countries to pass from their current underprivileged, distressed or depressed situation to a state of self-sustenance. Aid should provide countries with an opportunity to achieve steady, progressive growth. Economic aid should aim to make those to whom it is directed to organize themselves, to achieve a stable economy and to be autonomous with the result of the engagement. Suffice it to say no strings should be attached.

Nevertheless, though the above observation can uplift African countries, some, if not most African countries view Aid as merely another form of exploitation which will in some way benefit bigger and more powerful states outside Africa. Zimbabwe is one such suspicious nation that views foreign Aid as intentional motivations by the west to recolonise the country. This is oblivious of the concept of international co-operation and the inevitable creation of operational synergies required for the functioning of a global village. We call for sanity and sincerity on matters concerned with international affairs. Here we mean that the hard-won independence of the African states is still recent and these new nations raise alarm of suspicion of any aid coming from former colonial rulers. They think it is a " We give you and you obey us" relationship. But some African nations see grants from these big countries or organizations as a genuine effort for co-operation. (We may have to point out that Africa is abusing its thought matrices by missing the 'geography of spherical engagements'. For instance let us cite Zimbabwe as a case in point. The government adopted a "Look East" policy. Geographically they are not contented to watch their own feet. The Eastern countries also look to their East for developmental needs unavailable within their borders. Zimbabwe looks to China {East}, China looks to America {East} and America looks to Zimbabwe {East}, so where is East if not right there under our feet! Is it not a case of misplaced priorities and missing technological links that are needed to exploit and develop what we have into what we need!)

We have to note that our African states are still in the infancy of economic independence after years and decades of colonial rule, save for South Africa which has a developed transport and communication infrastructure comparable to those in Europe. It is widely agreed that African states in general fall short in funding themselves in different systems and to expand and diversify their economies hence the great need for aid. Revenues for African countries are too little to provide for development programmes, hence the need to supplement their fiscus with international loans and grants. It is evident that on their own, and in the near future, African states will never be in a better place to develop their own economies. Aid may come through grants, that is from developed countries and international bodies like the Breton Woods institutions.

A country should rely on what it generates but if it fails to meet its needs, then external Aid is needed. Foreign aid is meant to cover up the beneficiary countries' budget deficit. It finances part of the development of social services, capital development and the industry of that country. What is needed are principles that could be followed by a country on its development path. Growth of a country relies much on the networking and integration of different countries but not to be awkwardly dependent on foreign aid. African countries should therefore network with big industrialized nations in and outside the continent for developmental synergies.

This will suggest that there is need for adequate technical knowledge and skills in human capital in order to uplift Africa. Our personnel may have to undertake apprenticeships and internships in those engagements where they will gain more knowledge that is development directed. As well, we need educational opportunities to acquire competent experiences from around the world.

Countries in Africa are well capacitated with resources but Africans need an independence of the mind in order to transform these into meaningful wealth. What we experience is the abuse of these resources as they are channeled to fund political party activities instead of towards government programmes where all citizens get their share. Such cash cows as tourism, mining, exporting , manufacturing, telecommunications and agriculture can contribute towards shaping the country's economy, without allusions to imaginary geographic alignments. Each institution in a country should work hand and glove with any another to have a sustainable economic symbiosis.

It has to be noted out that a greater percentage of third world economies is generally dependent on inward external investment and aid. We get powerful countries gaining entrance to the resources of the African states as invited partners. This means that they have dividends from the investee countries on an agreeable and workable profit commutation matrix, they ship some and shape some, and shelve some too. If only Africa could explore ways to invest a greater percentage of the profits to sustainable priorities within the continent, it will realise sustainable growth and development that will cause it to transform from the begging bowl to a dishing spoon.

Africa is a continent with all resources that are needed but it fails to put contingent and concerted measures for international trade in order to beneficiate. Africa should not only wait for Aid but should wisely trade with other continents to appropriate its economy. We would buy the former British Prime Minister David Cameroon's view on his visit to Sub-Saharan South Africa that " trade, not aid would lift millions out of poverty"(**The daily news, African news,Tuesday July 19 2011,pg15**.) It is appreciable to be independent of foreign aid as many African states wish, but importantly we should revisit and improve the way we trade with other continents, however big and stubborn they may seem.

Trade is key to greater civilization. It gives potency to amity between peoples, especially when it flows freely under the guidance of mutual advantage and in response to dictates of market commands. A lot should be done by African countries to increase trade. New ideas should be embraced in order to achieve desired civilization. Thus, if there is need for new ideas, let them be researched, analysed, openly debated, validated, and systematically introduced. Any failure to introduce new systems in our governance structures means a deliberate failure to grow, hence our society will remain regressed. Hartley Withers in his book commented that, "If anyone would show us a better system that can be counted on with any certainty to lead us into a less ridiculous quagmire we should most of us be ready enough to work for its introduction" (**Everybody's business, Jonathan Cape limited, London.**) He continues to say that, "what a chance for a great increase in material comfort, and perhaps even for great advances towards a higher and nobler civilization, with poverty and destitution abolished , and contentment and co-operation spread like rich manure over the surface " (Ibid pg 288.)

People should not look up to non-governmental organisations for help while they are still strong and able to work. Leaders should work and strive to educate their younger generations to prioritise and cherish the importance and contribution of the dignity of labour. People should work and not wait for Aid! This is a nag, a syndrome. People fail to appreciate their hands as the best, if not only, Aid they have ever had. Our hands help us to work and produce. What great Aid do we need from other people than our own hands! The dexterity of our fingers is the mother of all human Aid. Aid should not be given to lazy people, but to those who wish their projects to be supported and boosted, except only in extreme cases of war, disaster or famine, otherwise aid will fail its meaning. Many people who wish for help are not supposed to get it unless we intent to create a community of lazy people. A great nation is born from great workers, who involve and engage themselves in the day to day undertakings of their communities, both individually and collectively. On-lookers and backbenchers should be vehemently condemned. Whose food do they wish to table, just to ask? We lament that a time will come when the constitutions will recommend that those found lazing around be made to work in companies and factories or even in some form of productive service. Africa should be aware of its potency and encourage itself to have confidence in its capacity to bring about a better desired future.

Gerroh Michalitsiano in his book **Extracting Value** wrote that "Africa's vast mineral deposits make it, arguably, the world's greatest treasure chest. Africa contains around 85% of the world's chromium and platinum as a well more than 60% of the reserves of cobalt and manganese. It ranks either first or second with her reserves of diamonds, bauxite, phosphate rocks, vermiculite and chromium. Africa also produces more than 21% of the world's gold, 16% of its uranium and 13% of its petroleum. Naturally mineral exploitation and production constitute significant parts of the economies of a number of African countries and they remain key to the future economic growth of this developing continent." He was also quick to point out the inefficiencies of the continent saying, "It is also home to some of the best examples of poor social stewardship and unregulated environmental impact on record. Most of the countries classified as least developed in the greater global context, are African" One is more than tempted to agree with Gerroh's conclusions. Africa should capitalize on its resources in order to boost and overhaul its economy. The statistics shown above by Michalitsiano are informative. He went on to point out that one of the greatest challenges facing African leaders is lack of proper strategies, policies and programmes   that ensure the mining of mineral resources becomes an important avenue for sustainable economic growth and development in their individual and collective states. Africa is facing challenges while it is seated on untapped wealth. He concluded sighting countries like Zimbabwe where he said is facing an economic onslaught by its own home grown covert politicians.

Africans and their countries have too many resources but they need to be transformed into wealth. This will curb dependency on other continents, and create interdependent synergies instead. Several contributions have been penned that carry in them both political and economic intelligence to help the Africa of today to construct a better tomorrow for itself, but, alas, these suggestions are overturned by corrupt leaders who suspect them as an attempt at their sovereignty. However, the best of leaders allow such pointers a place in the policy making primeval soup, and need we suggest more!

7 ON REMAKING AFRICAN HISTORY

The history of a people defines them. The African people are defined by the political, social, economic and religious status which they found themselves in.

An eye on the colonial era would tell that the means of production remained largely for and with the colonizers. Large companies, like De Beers or Anglo American from big economies, controlled the African economy. All profits from these multinational companies were commuted back to their founders' home countries, although some exploitation from and within the African countries was really evident.

For now we cannot hold that when the colonial traders came, they robbed the Africans. The Martians did not intent for a loot but prosperity. They only went around the world looking for opportunities. Otherwise, they came to share some light of their extraterrestrial wisdom with Earthens, or are they Africans? But, unfortunately, some of the colonizers ill-treated the innocent Earthen men for no reasonable cause. Africans were therefore ill-treated and got no retribution.

Nevertheless, we cannot still dwell on the cruelties and injustices of the past. Doing so will drive us into despair. Let us be just visionaries, looking further ahead. There is much opportunity, much potential and intelligence in the African people. There is much wealth in our minerals, with our fertile lands and the human capital, we need only to put ourselves together and readdress our situation. Our confidence and effort should grow in fashioning ourselves towards the love for prosperity. A prosperity which will guarantee us a better tomorrow. Our vision should be moulded in the form of solidarity among the different individuals and ethnic groups, among institutes and states, the basis being LOVE, which conquers divisions and brushes off all the superiority/inferiority complexities. We love this community and united we can work to build it. Our predicament? Our failures in the economic sector, or even in our politics, can never be attributed to colonialism but to our failure to be self motivated, disciplined, and organized .
.

Yes, we still have much to understand about colonialism. During the time of colonialism Africans knew less of the international markets and the global undertakings. Later there was a shift of power into black hands. Blacks failed to fully utilise what they were left with, from their colonizers. The industry and the services dwindled with time. Some of the black elites began to milk the profits of the nations to their personal gain. They had no new ideas based on their African ideologies, but instead banked on farfetched, borrowed speculations, only to follow the colonial traditional understanding of the economy, and, even politics. They then followed their former colonial masters to their countries with a big begging bowel, demanding retribution. What made the blacks fight against colonization was the identification of the weaknesses of the colonizers who jeopardized the African dignity and treated them as second class citizens who should be subservient to the Martian and Babylonian Brotherhood. But, we notice that some of our leaders are on the fore-front perpetrating acts against human dignity. Colonizers gave orders (measures) that threatened many and killed a few. The indegenous oppressors threaten many and also kill many more. Local contemporary oppressors are more dangerous and more ruthless. Think of the Rwanda genocide, what about the bloody Zimbabwe Gukurahundi in mid 80^s, the Egyptian and Libyan hard-handedness against the Arab spring and so on.

To strive forward, Africans need to have a common interest where they can built an African sovereignty with one political   leadership and with one currency. We cannot remain in the cocoon of weaknesses, feeling warm in retarded progress and a blinkered view in industry. No one wishes Africa to remain at where it is or continuing to have a very low and slow rate of growth being 'enjoyed' at the moment. We need a transformation of the African society into a modern industrial state. There is not much effectiveness in continuously giving reference and emphasis on how Africa got to be liberated from colonial rule, but rather more to the need to work for a balanced economic growth pathway. In case our leaders are scared to lead large populations as would happen in the event of an African Union of States, they had better advise themselves to take leaves off the Chinese and Indian states whose individual populations are far larger than the combined population of Africa.

8 ON ECONOMIC MIGRATION

There is also a phenomenon of people crossing borders to seek employment in neighbouring and even faraway countries. Migrants wish to find opportunities for a better life. It is a fairly well established fact that labour migration fluctuates correspondingly to the success or failure of a country's economic performance. This is true when a country is under a failed government which pursues ill-conceived principles to the regress of the national fiscus, or if the country has been hit by civil war or by other economic problems. In this case migrants to other countries increase, but if things are good then emigrant numbers will decrease. The fact that labour migration falls away if the country has been sound or if alternative economic opportunities open up, suggests that the number of migrants from a particular country is, in fact, on one hand, a balance between economic needs and on the other hand, a certain national constraint. Thus, if a country's economic opportunities improve, the country restraints or keeps the worker in one's country, but if conditions deteriorate, and the economic needs of the local people cannot be met, then it will lead to an increased rate of emigration. Economic migration is not a phenomenon that can be controlled willy-nilly by rules and regulations. It can only be reversed by a country's deliberate creation of a vibrant economy. What lies behind a peculiar characteristic of labour migration is the ability of the country to offer itself sustainable growth, and nothing more.

9 ON FUSION TO ONE NATION

Kwameh Nkrumah was the first African President. He led Ghana to independence in 1958. This was the first crack to dispel the colonial rule in the entire Africa. African independent rule was from then felt across the continent, but mainly in the central to the north and west of Africa. The hallmark of African independence was for the equal sharing of the resources (that all have worked for together). This means that African independence was a cause to bridge the gap between many disparities in the society. It was to create a society devoid of racism, that is, a society with one people, of the one heart, and with different duties.

Being independent from the colonial rule was a step ahead for Africans. They now could occupy better jobs which they could not land under colonial rule.

In the African mind, by getting independence they thought they would fly an aeroplane the next day. They thought they would easily build themselves better houses in suburbs where colonial masters lived. They perceived themselves as the next black-white man or white-black man.

This did not come out true because on ascending to governance, most African leaders proved to be too thinly minded for the job. They proved not equipped enough to implement what could improve the folk. It was never in their veins to manage sophisticated governance procedures and structures. In fact, they were not patient to be inducted, and therefore depended solely on theorized college learnings coupled with imagined practicalizations.

If the founding fathers in the 1960s had worked a surface clean up, we remain skeptic that a groundbreaking effort could have been made towards unity as was the will behind the pan-African project. Only if Kwameh Nkrumah and other early first presidents had organized that all the countries which also eventually won independence would combine to become one province and its leader by default be Nkrumah, also by default, all countries would have been made to join in. It pays to remember that during the scramble for Africa colonizers shared different portions from a united Africa. Portions were either under the French or the Germans, with the British, Portuguese, Spaniards and other European negotiators at the Berlin indaba rushing in for their fair shares. The colonizers, however, surrendered these portions at different periods. Northern Africa was early in the 60s, that was to be submitted by the French while the Southern part like Zimbabwe by the Britons later in the 80s, with South Africa gaining freedom in the mid 90s. This was a deliberate strategy that ensured the African provinces would not unite as immediately as would make them formidable. The Africans were made to mistrust each other and to maintain their distances with respect to the instilled thought of republics that are autonomous and independent of each other. At that time Europe itself was regrouping into the EU, getting prepared for an eventual invasion by a united Africa. Would it not hold much water if the African people noticed that Europe divided them so as not to rule them, but rather it was scared! Very much afraid, influenced by their observation that the African mind was full of hate and rage! We should think so. Very much so!

It could have been a big leap only if the countries which had cut the chains of colonialism to have united with Ghana and other already formed states in the making of one big block that would have one president. All the representatives of all to-be liberated countries would then act as executive governors of their new states presided over by one African leader. That was to be more nationalistic, more pan-africanist, greater ubuntu! The chance went quietly unnoticed. What was important during the formative years of African independence was naturally to form a union where a single leadership would be identified.

Our first African leaders, such as Nkrumah, would have gone farther than only forming a Pan African Freedom Movement of East and Central Africa, but to form an African Union where every single country would come in as a province with a governor of that province elected by the people. More would have come from such a continental movement, rather than a narrowly impoverished certain country or a small movement. We have to think of why the Soviet Union or the USA combined to form one state. Now we have Europe. It was not as a game plan to win some tournament or outplay each other, but rather to muscle up in order to engage in wider scope to fight the calamites that threaten life, such as diseases, hunger or border conflicts, and as well to pool resources, capital, skills and technologies towards one common cause beneficial to all.

We should acknowledge very well that during this period of African neo-colonialism, Africa was just emerging from a different world. They were in our zone enjoying life in the villages and had the administration under a tree. But the type of administration was different. It was now the top floor administration which needed a jointing of the African concept and mind.

The blocks we currently have in Africa like SADC or ECOWAS are a pointer to the significance of coming together as one group to make life sustainable. If only the countries which had won independence in different parts of Africa combined to make one African block! This block would be one from Cape to Cairo under one president and with one currency. The different countries would then be turned into provinces. Then each province would also be demarcated into smaller area-specific local governance constituencies. From these provinces there would be representatives who would be elected by the people. These governors would help the president in parliament as the cabinet to run the affairs of the African Block. Local issues would be resolved and implementation carried out on a provincial level by the governor of that province. Those issues which would require a bigger, broader and stronger magnitude (panel) would be resolved by the governors of different provinces together with the president of Africa. Devolution would be the guide principle.

The future of Africa may remain bleak and may create more damage, with a face of poverty, with wars its morning after-pill. Unless solutions equal to the problems on the ground are formulated and implemented to wade off the ever growing problems in the sorry state of our Africa, we will continue to enjoy lamentations.

A solution may come through the integration of the African states. What is needed is for these small underdeveloped nations to quickly integrate to one nation state. As one nation, Africa then is able to plan its economies at a larger level. On their own, these states may fail to create a viable economy. These individual states are economically unbalanced. They should combine and be stronger in their effort for investment. Countries in Africa should regroup themselves on an economic basis and act in communion.

A general valuable pattern of integration among different neigbouring states has come up as ECOWAS or SADC but is still remote in its dealings. The United States of Africa should be formed to remove trade barriers among African countries thus enhancing the growth of the economy in Africa.

Change in the African continent rests with the Africans. The change we want is in our hands. Everyone should be engaged in changing for the better. Africa should embrace opportunities and combine its forces to combat poverty.

Hope is there for Africa to develop labour-intensive methods of industrialization. Our need is to have a united people who have no demarcations that will hinder great economic production. Cape to Cairo is a blessed place with all that is desired to make life of the African better.

With such large quantities of gold in South Africa, diamonds in Botswana and more reserves of coal in Western Africa. Zimbabwe also holds a lot of these wealth reserves with its agricultural base and one of the best ethanol plant in Africa. We have oil deposits within African soil and water beds, hence amalgamating countries of Africa under one distinct government is a great leap forward, considering the suffering of the African people, despite our vast and diverse natural resources.

The failures by different countries to sustain their economies is an indication towards a radical paradigm shift in the desire for a change in the whole set up of the continent. This is evidenced by the low quality of life where most are in need of the basic needs and services. A united community is of necessity since everything would be shared across the African land and that would enhance the life status of many.

This focused intergovernmental organization, with one leader, will be in a position to promote unity and solidarity amongst these African states. More to this is that it would spur economic development. Central or pivotal to all this development would be the resolution of conflict thu offering guarantees for peace and stability among states. This principal organ, probably made of governors of provinces, would create a mechanism to engage in peacemaking on the continent. Boundary conflicts would be abolished, citizens would be exculpated on issues of illegal citizenship. Through this there would be no boundary but one nation of several provinces, tribes, races and religions. It would be one nation of people with one identity, same aim, goal and geared for the same achievement. If this could come out as a reality, it would be a major practical achievement where border disputes e.g. in Rwanda, Somalia, could be closely monitored and be dealt with effectively, as each province would be absolved from territorial encroachment.

It would be a major boost on the premise of trade and development. One of the objects to occupy the heart of this organ would be to lessen poverty and bring affluence among Africans. This shows that by nature it would be both economic and social. It would be economic in the sense that the wealth of Africa would be evenly distributed among the states. People would access industrial sites to work in without the hassle for visas and passports. Recurrent expenditure in terms of executive salaries would be greatly reduced. Imagine that currently Africa pays more than 50 presidents, thousands of ministers and parliamentarians who gobble a sizeable chunk of GDP. The use of a single currency would ease and encourage interprovincial commodity exchange transactions. Of great importance would be central commodity broking and trade between Africa and her outside neighbours. This would reduce the risk of exploitation by those who kept dividing us for that purpose. It is needless to mention the obvious that the African currency would be stronger than the competing world currencies, we do not want to consider ourselves as speculators on this one.

It would be social in the sense that there would be a sense of brotherhood created by being a people of the same nation. In effect, that was the Africa before the invasion by settlers from elsewhere.

Another aim would be to enlist Africans to the cause of the continental peace and development and then take off to the global platform. Africa should not be scared to implement changes. If it fails then we may ask if Africa is too powerless to effect change or too powerful to be constrained by it.

To acquire a better Africa we may implore some socialistic ideas. "Socialism is based on a respect for human beings, for all persons whatever their age, sex, race, creed or work". Our goal is to share the African riches equally and equitably. What is produced should benefit all. The fruits of labour should be for all.

Socialism seeks also to respect the dignity of the human person, safeguard his or her freedom and provide the environment for the full moral and cultural fulfillment of everyone in the community. Socialism is egalitarian and communitarian. Human efforts should not fall short of such a high ideal. The values and priorities of socialism should be upheld. Socialism can be described as basal to better and growing economies.

Apart from succeeding to maintain peace and stability, there are also other significant objectives to consider, such as developing friendly relations among the provinces and states based on respect for the principles of equal rights and self-determination of their peoples. Above all, it is to achieve a workable platform for a worldwide co-operation to solve international economic, social, cultural and humanitarian problems.

Human rights have to be held in uppermost hand in the African states. This is because human rights are painfully frustrated by social forces, resulting in exploitation, oppression, persecution and other forms of deprivation and segregation. Human rights are rights enshrined 'in' an individual or group of individuals as a consequence of being human. They refer to a wide continuum of values or capability in order to enhance human agency and declared to be universal in character. Human rights serve as a centre where people can co-ordinate their actions and activities towards various ends.

10 ON BECOMING AND CULTURE

No one would like to remain a child. We need to grow and achieve a total personality. Total growth is necessitated and cultivated in early childhood. A child should get opportunities for expression, due freedom and not be exposed to very rigid disciplinary controls augmented by harsh punishments. When a child grows up with such kind of opportunities, there are greater chances of producing a creative person. Children pass through different stages to be fully grown, thus from infancy, childhood to adolescence as developmental genetic psychology suggests. Each developmental stage has its own characteristics. It is most proper that society be aware of, and conversant with, the characteristics of each stage and make use of this knowledge in giving proper instruction and guidance to properly modify the behavior and intellectual capacities of the child.(Unfortunately the scope of these epistles does not accommodate a detailed discussion of developmental psychology as this is a preserve for career practitioners. We shall however skim over contributions that are just right for our purpose)

In trying to answer how a person grows, Sigmund Freud analysed it with his theory of personality. He stated that "psychoanalysis is dynamic and based on the assumption that personality and personality development are determined by conflicts and events that are largely unconscious in nature" However Alfred Adler who was Sigmund's disciple refuted the above assertion saying that self-assertion rather than sex impulse is the major drive. He put it forcefully that, "Human behaviour was determined not by the biological forces of instinct but by social forces and social attitudes and interests are determined through learning experiences" Freud emphasizes the role of the unconscious to influence the person. Adler specified the conscious saying that it anticipates the future goals which influence the present behavior.

In this case we may be swallowed in the psychology of Adler. We must be very aware of, and be on high alert on, the way we have taught the child. The child on its side assimilates the values, the ideas, and the morality of the authority which is from its society. The child values what the society tested, proved, did and put in its system. The child has to shape up with the society's way of thinking, because the child's growth is largely instructed by the structure of the society, and less from the individual himself, hence, a close monitoring of its growth is needed. This means that even the schools the children attend have a function and responsibility to them.

The child should be helped. Helping the child to have liberty in thinking will enhance his position in the society as he grows. This will prevent the child from being exploited and oppressed. The values and belief system should necessarily guide the children in later life to be producers of the state-of-the-art ideas. This gives one a leverage and privilege within his colleagues, and removes stigma and concealment from and within other members of the same society. This is the panacea against exploitation and oppression. All this claims that we must produce a society which is upright in order for it to up bring children of the desired calibre, who can be tested and proven by the same standards and instruments available in the same society.

Now looking at culture, the African condition should oversee this. Culture plays a very important role in shaping the future of a person. Culture has its unique power over our thinking. Its natural unique power has been complicated by the multi-cultural sub-societies from which we grow. Some are trapped up in the sense that they learn other languages as they grow. Learning a language is at the same time learning the culture expressed by that language, hence, being good at other languages is verisimilitude to being good at their respective cultures.

Now that we grow up in a culture, we need to be much aware of some aspects of the respective cultures which positively shape our future and identify those that are negatively skewed. As Africans, we need to grow. We are still to gain the stability needed to consolidate learnings from our failures. We know who we are, we know what we want! We have to look at our culture to find areas that may need improvement and re-shaping. Every culture is indeed rich, but at the same time needs refashioning in some aspects in order to keep in tandem with transformations within and without it.

The African culture has power over our thinking. If we go down to its semiotics we get its real effects on today's African thinking in a variety of ways.

In pre-historic times the instincts were a force over the life and activities of the primitive peoples. Their simple life was basically food and sex. What preserved the instincts and what propagated them was most paramount. Life was viewed under the two instincts, that is self-propagation and self-preservation. Today we also notice these instincts in play in the African man. More to this was that man lived in a brute way of invading and killing other tribes. Thomas Hobbes analysed the primitive man and conclusively viewed him as bad. He wrote in his book **Leviathan** that man is a ferocious animal. Man is a wolf to his neighbour (Homo homini lupus) He continued to say that man is a killer at heart, he is against the society.

A contemporary man would be tempted to describe the current African as he would describe the semiotic man. Fighting in Africa is a means (and a bad one at that) that has engulfed the minds of most of us in order to pirate the riches of others.

No one wants war! No one wants fighting, but the loathness under our hearts and the love for riches make us to be ruthless. In essence, we should work in order to prosper, rather than to kill for it. We should not see work as a burden but to glorify it in order to progress. We should not progress through brutal means but through labour. We should see our community as a labouring society. If we work, produce and share the fruits, we will be the happiest people on the planet, considering that we are a happy people despite our poverty and synthetic troubles and arduous struggles.

The condition we have plunged ourselves in is pitiful. Let us fight earnestly against this condition which we have brought forward to ourselves or found ourselves in. Our minds are confined to food, drink and sex as dictated by our instincts. In Africa we find ourselves being interested in politics just because there is a food ration or hamper gotten after chanting party slogans.

This goes badly here in Rwanda where a boy in his teens would hold the trigger in the middle of the bush. Man has no sympathy with his fellow. Think of Boko Haram here in Nigeria. The greater virtues of truth, justice and goodness were and are still being ignored. These values, if allowed to prevail in peoples' lives, will lay the foundation on which sound relationships and a community of collegiality will be formed and established.

After this basically primitive life of instinctual drive whose only raison d'être hinged on reproducing and preserving life, people began to engage in regulating desired habits to form customs or religions. Also, were taboos, rituals and the force of the mass(vox populi vox credint), they were caught much in the natural tendencies of imitativeness and suggestibility. These collective tendencies are much at play in today's Africa. We are so closely knit that, as was said by one philosopher, "what I am is because we are." An individual's life affects the whole community or the tribe positively or negatively. Customs arise when certain practices satisfy the instinctive craving lives. But still by doing all this have we attained the status of life demanded of us? Not yet, we presume. Does charity, justice, peace and economic empowerment cascade from certain customs? We have to embrace them if ever they do.

The elaborate religious practices really add awe and authority to peoples' lives, yes; but do they emancipate man from the constraints of the contemporary African man hoodwinked in undergrowth and large margins of under civilization? Africans are so custom ridden that trivial issues may be given magnanimous importance, hence stalling the movement forward. People are congregated in their aloofness, waiting for a ritual to commence and thereafter feel life's story has been accomplished. We should not wait for some miraculous sign for us to move forward. We are the miracle, the mind is the sign, it will move us ahead. Man and women of Africa should strive and struggle to set goals and keep sighing for higher goals and desires such as peace, justice and economic boost.

A breakthrough is needed where an African renaissance is achieved, an emancipation of thought and action that leads us to discard the soiled past and offers avenues to a fresher African future. We must shed off the conservatism and the fundamentalism acculturated into us by our former colonial masters and proceed to encompass a total decolonization and liberation of the mind. Africa still has to develop. Africa has to develop and endure relationships among itself and other continents. It is this culture that we have to aspire for our children, and constantly inure them thereto!

11 ON LEADERSHIP

Leadership in Africa has taken a different view as to what has to be universally understood of the term. Leadership is about serving, rather than being served. There has been, in Africa, a totalitarian concept of leadership. This is one factor that has made the continent go down to regression. This is very unfortunate. One who is voted for by the majority, would refuse to let go when it is time to step down. This is reminiscent of a dictatorship. Leaders over enjoy the benefits associated with their positions. The case is that if one is voted into power, no sooner does he forget those who put him to that position of power. The leaders seem to profess in public that the nation means all the people, yet at the back of their minds and imaginations the nation is distinctively viewed as exclusively theirs, effectively ignoring the living fact that any country is the people's republic. Unless our leaders in Africa undergo a profound transformation from this mindset, and a change in their hearts, it will be difficult for them to admit the people's place in the affairs of the nation as agents of progressive development and industrialization. Our continent risks being blocked from growth and becoming impoverished, if it does not encourage the participation of, and by all. The principle of subsidiarity in governance should be given centre stage.

A reading from the gospel of Mathew chapter 7 verses 15,18-20 encourages everyone to work more fervently. It says that "Beware of false prophets, who come to you in sheep's clothing, but inwardly are ravenous wolves ….. a good tree that cannot produce good fruits is cut down and thrown into the fire. So then you will know them by their fruits" Leaders in some African countries come to the people campaigning, proclaiming to help and develop the society if it elects them. Little does the community know that deep down the candidate's heart there is more of personal aggrandisement than self sacrifice. They long for wealth and all that measures up to good life, even if it is on the expense of the people. This is in context when Jesus said that if a tree fails to produce good fruits the electorate should not delay use of the fire. A bad leader cannot produce good results for his people. These leaders, as Jesus said that if a tree fails to produce good fruits, then it has to be cut down and thrown into the fire. Also bad leaders need to be replaced! If a leader has eventually shown evidence of their incompetence, it suffices to hold peaceful demonstrations to alert the leader about the people's discontentment. Demonstrations are bad if they turn violent and destroy property and in the process injure, maim or kill people. Demonstrations are a constitutional avenue to express displeasure. The security officers are there only to monitor the venues and rendezvous where the demonstrations will take place. If a leader fails to meet the people's expectations then he has to step down. Stepping down is by no means humiliation, but is a sign of humility. Humility means going down to accept reality. So leaders should learn to face reality and be happy to act accordingly and responsibly.

When the president fails the country's economy, then one should let go. Stepping down willingly is a sign of maturity, growth and love for the nation. If one steps down, one goes with honour. Our leaders have to grow. It is disgusting that some will cling to power for periods exceeding those proclaimed by the constitution. They must know that before their tenure some leaders had led the same country. Even after them other leaders will follow, maybe of a better calibre and quality. The country does not necessarily need you, one is never indispensable because any capable person can do the job, and even better. Everyone is just contingent. No one is a necessity. On any leadership post there are too many possible candidates. It is only that we cannot occupy the same office at the same time. But be aware that what you are, many a man can also be. African leaders who fail their countries' economies and remain in power are likened to the allegory which was given by the Zimbabwean erudite politician Dr Edson Zvobgo. He narrated of a village idiot from Ngomahuru Psychiatric Centre who, once handed the button stick in a relay race, ran astray into the hills with it, away from the track and never handed it to the next runner resulting in the whole team losing the race. Surely, we know that for a team to win, the button stick has to be handed to the next athlete. Zvobgo was of course right, He spoke figuratively of African despots who have largely been afflicted by the Ngomahuru virus or syndrome and who once they get into office and become leaders, lock the door from inside and flush the key down the toilet. These despots do not see beyond themselves, they think that without them, their countries would fall apart. Respected leader Woodrow Wilson warned that power corrupts and absolute power corrupts absolutely. He aptly observed that leaders who do not perceive a future without them are a liability to society.

However these governance intelligences fall on deaf ears.

It is not pleasing in Africa because at any given epoch we have leaders who manipulate the people. Leaders should not exploit the people. No manipulative cutthroat practices should be tolerated. Some leaders do this to further their own vested interests. When these leaders address in public, they promise high-sounding love and cooperation ideals. But all these public pronouncements about peace, love, unity and harmony are a mask that disappears after the event. What we need in Africa are peacemaking leaders. It is so painful that our leaders find advantage in the misfortune of our fellow men and that one man's loss almost always translates to another man's wealth. This made Jean-Jacques Rousseau to comment that man has hardly any troubles except those he has given himself.

Now hearken to the wailing souls you leaders of the land. The people in their bounds look up to you, but you dare not turn. Even if you do not turn to them, they still will love you for the persons you are, and they will still dance, cheering you up to deliver the promises offered in your manifestos. Please leaders, love and help these poor country-men.

The leader, the fortunate one, rises from the bed in the morning as the sun rises from the east. The leader smiles, looking at the labouring countrymen in his fields. On the back of his mind he smatters, 'my slaves'. We are ashamed of our leaders who feel warm in this coat of wickedness. When you bed these leaders, you have bedded the spouse of danger, fiancés of corruption. Their eyes are ruthless. No feel of warmth comes from their hands, but 'loot and shoot'. They come down to the rural areas, to the humble of soul, to the smooth vein of peace, where love and humility streams, to a people who have won nothing in life but a stuff. What matters for this country man is his fill, not the foreign language. Culture and tradition stand at his door but the civilization of foreign lands is still apart. We see this country-man, gliding under the mountain trees, tending the cattle and sheep. He enjoys nature, talking to it, all moments with serenity insulating his thoughts. Please leaders do not trouble this man.

Africa needs leaders who understand! Understanding is a great tool to simplify problems. To solve problems, we need to first understand the gaps. In this way, we manipulate the conflicting variables to produce the correct response. For this to happen we do not only need educated leaders, but leaders who are open to the ideas of others. We need leaders who do not give way to cultural, political, racial or class differences, leaders who are true to themselves and to the rest of the world, who are compassionate and honest with their words and deeds. This will increase harmony among the leaders and the people, thus perpetuating a better understanding and create ideas equal to the challenges of our time, eventually leading to solutions of our problems. In this way we can then achieve the goals all await.

Leaders of today should not be so adamant when appending on treaties, and, from those treaties emerging with more guns. People want food not guns. On the height of an epidemic or famine we observe governments expending on guns. Please leaders sell the guns and buy food for the starving people.

It is a fact that the burden which the worker shoulders in Africa has necessitated an exodus to European and other countries. They have lost hope and faith in the leaders they have elected. The question to the worker is, how the unjust situation can be changed so that a basis for a better economy can be achieved. The other problem is that the worker finds two options to take at the same time, locked in Scylla and Charybdis. On one hand he has to jump over the border to seek refuge in other countries, labeled as greener pastures, on the other hand to remain in the country and suffer under a clueless and brutal leadership. This is the trauma of the contemporary African. Actually this is particularly true of the young and middle aged. Those who are young cross the border to other countries while they are still strong to make hay. But it will not be good to presume that these youngsters do not have a patriotic sense for their nationalities. We strongly believe that it is often the sense of irrelevance, futility, and the lack of an identity in their respective countries that leads them to move away from their countries. The populace hardly sees themselves as relevant to the overall economic or social change. The general absence of dynamism in leadership within those who lead the country adds much to this. The worker feels deceived by different leaders who have taken the people to the present mess. The labourer endures brute, while the leader profits.

However, let us say that the people are the authors of their destiny. They get an opportunity to elect their leaders during plebiscites but what do they do? They assign hyenas to take care of their livestock and when the sheep are consumed they wonder why! While in parliament, the people's representatives fear to give a vote of no confidence to underperforming executives, let alone impeach the presidium for maladministration and other unconstitutional misdemeanors. Africa rise up to conscience against partisan conscience collectif!

12 ON DEMOCRACY IN AFRICA

Is democracy in Africa real? Many African countries are still being ruled by autocratic regimes masquerading as revolutionary institutions, although they claim to be independent. Many African leaders proclaim to be democratic although there are evident signs that they neither safeguard it nor uphold the principles upon which a democratic state is formed. We should spell out that democracy is not only about majority rule, but also the respect and protection of minority rights. The question still remains, do we have it in Africa? Democracy demands peace and truceful power transitions. Before we discuss democracy, let us come to contain what peace is, so that we understand its relationship to democracy

Peace is not only the absence of war and all its concomitant threats, but a condition where all universal human rights are upheld without fear or favour. It means the equality of persons before the law. It further requires the respect and preservation of cherished values and the support of democratic institutions and principles. It is about freedom and independence of our various social constitutions within a framework of agreed non-suppressive democratic processes. It is about humanity and all its cherished wills. The question still comes back, do we have it in Africa? It translates to no peace no democracy and vice versa!

In the traditional African cultural context, democratic people have relationships of solidarity, sharing and the formation of one big community. They are not just individuals living, but individuals who are tightly knit together. In a democracy, economic and social justice prevail, making it possible for people to enjoy a decent life and to have access to essential services. A democratic country or community respects and promotes human rights both within and without its borders. "Democracy is understood to mean putting in place conditions and structures that make it possible for people to live in peace and harmony while respecting individual and cultural differences" (**F Wilfred and Iniz Carlos, Christianity and Democracy,pg 83, SusinScim Press, London, 2007**.)

In the different African countries what is needed is the government of the people, by people and for the people. What is important is to discover its essence and implement it in the African states. What we know to be democracy in our intellectual circles and in the treaties on the science of governance should be merged with the action thereto expected. If there is no correspondence between the two then it becomes a farce. There is need to walk the talk. From an epistemological point of view, if we cannot reconcile what is on the ground (real) and what we apprehend in our minds, then this disparity shows a deficiency in our performance since we cannot reconcile the two. Democracy stems from respecting oneself and also respecting the position which one has acquired from the populace. The people have voted you to lead them, hence they need respect in reciprocation. Democracy also comes as loving the nation and the maintenance of its resources for the perpetuity of future generations.

Democracy should be compatible with human dignity and social viability. The governments in Africa frustrate the citizens because they dismally fail to fulfill the promises they make during the run up to elections. The leaders should be implored to tow the line with regards to democracy. Each government should have institutionalised tools of checks and balances in order to moderate its internal and external functions. With checks and balances in government, the aim will be to put a form of polyarchy, allowing structural constraints to ensure republics are not converted to monarchs.

Most governments in Africa claim they follow the concept of democratic centralism where in which all ideas are generated from the executive and cascaded down to the electorate for directed debate. This ensures that the ruling ideas are indeed the ideas of the ruling elite. This disregards the input from the people. It assumes that those in government know what is best for the people. This creates strongmen who end up encircled by a highly protective network of securocrats. It effectively puts the leader in the position of ruler and guarantees his superiority over the rest of the citizenry. In fact, the concept of democratic pluralism has not been part of African traditional governance systems where the power of patriarchs remain unchallenged. With the adoption of western type of government, Africans are advised to adapt to the inherited institution unless they wish to mismanage the affairs of their lands. One cannot run a modern economy on archaic processes and procedures. It has to dawn on every leader's mind that the people know better what is best for them. Participatory leadership styles are in tandem with modern trends in today's dynamic societies. Escaping this observation invites anarchy to our social corridors, no wonder the uprisings and civil strife bedeviling many countries. It is not that Africans do not understand democratic pluralism, they just do not have the will power to implement it, hence they tend to understate it. In short, leaders are too corrupt to be any sincere, they fear the people who elected them because they are rarely clean. The choice to centralize government operations is aimed at obliterating the relevance of the minds of the electorate. The people are exposed to silhouettes of the truth. But the demand for democracy remains to haunt all governments forever, despite iron hand tactics to suppress it. Arise, Africa, arise!

13 ON RESHAPING THE SOCIETAL POSITION OF WOMAN

There has to be special recognition for women's active participation in all institutions. Women in Africa have been denied most of their basic human rights, although they shoulder heavy responsibilities in the home and society. Recently, a step in the right direction has been deliberately taken to recognize societal balance in gender relations. It has to be noted and emphasized that gender equality should be a done debate. But today, women are struggling for emancipation from male chauvinistic pigs who hold on tightly to dehumanising perceptions against the women folk. Women themselves are confident and assure themselves to be mature people with a voice worth listening to. They are our pillars in the society. The Almighty has bestowed on them what men and themselves need in order to spark the fire of a well-polished society and guarantee enormous lifelong initiatives.

A woman's consciousness of herself must be widened and

deepened to occupy substantial space in the socio-economic and political structures of society. Women must not only be seen on the lower profiles of society but should also decide to engage in its growth. Engaging in such matters would categorically define their level of achievement in the society.

Men and women should complement each other to produce the most favourable conditions for symbiotic existence. Complementarity implies equality. Women should deny a coordinated oppression and the systematic exploitation laid upon them by the systems of a historically patriarch modeled society. Women oppression could easily be overcome if we come to understand that men and women share the same resources, for the same purpose and same life, and that we are all created to negotiate interdependence. We should say no to the shrewdness provided by class exploitation employed to maintain the domination of women by their very product –men!. Our men need awareness on such defining matters.

Gender inequality and gender inequity stem from the myriad forms of injustices provided for by our constitutions. African lands have been known to be a soil which has to be presided over by a male figure, with historical convention proving it as the 'Land of the patriarchs!' Women were or are still uninvited to matters of worth in the African setup. In some nations, women do not own land in their own right, while in others all they do has to be approved by the men, even if they are not their husbands. Remotely, but commonly done, is the practice of sacrificing virgins to appease the gods and avenging spirits. In the home, women are reduced to vessels of sexual pleasure created to satisfy the male ego, and their enjoyment of the game is not an issue. In religious congregations women are recipients of the word and songbirds whose voices bring harmony to the hymnals, as if to lull God.

The different feminist movements advancing gender equality discourse are fighting hard for change. Proposals have been tabled whose agenda is to uplift the women in society. Yes, one may be feministic in all earnest but it does fail to help if those who are advocated for fail to show up. Women should stand up and show strength in all avenues available in society. The female voices should be heard from all corners and with powerful force. Women's liberation, that is, the actual change of attitude by men towards women is the goal. We need an increasing number of women fire fighters, pure science scholars (students) and in politics, not only to sing and ululate on campaign rallies and in churches led by men.

The African women have for quite some time been submerged to homemaking and babysitting qualifications. But to date, they have come to realize and be realized away from the embryonic stage, marching to the pinnacle of academic and economic diligence. The more women appreciate their passions and their intelligence in their respective societies, the more they bring their imaginations to reality. Men are men, only when they accept women as working warriors in this weird world. But it is not for the sympathizer to do everything for the people they are fighting for, but those so regarded have to put up their girdles and go! Unfortunately, most women do not trust their capacities and those of their counterparts. Ironically, pit a man against a woman, get the surprise of many women recommending a man. This change of attitude is what is left for the African woman to do! It is noteworthy that progressive societies have embraced the Beijing Convention's calls for gender equality by putting in place positive discrimination mechanisms which allow for quota allocation of posts to be reserved for women as a way of boosting confidence in the woman. Let us maintain we remain equal and level the ground to allow for gender balance. What remains unequal, out of all purposes, is the marriage chores which were preordained from procreation. This has been the worry for the African man who saw his role as family head under threat as some women overdid the women's liberation claims and challenged their spouses to change roles in the house- husbands found it difficult to get pregnant, even if they might have wanted!

14 ON PENURY

Many any African state has large masses of poor people within its borders. In some better of nations we still find the poor pocketed within the fringes of the metropolitan cities. These are the people who are exploited by the rich in society. They provide cheap labour, line up to vote, taken to serve in the emergency army units, and women are raped or forced into prostitution. This is alarming, but leaders seem to give a blind eye and deaf ear to their plight.

International emissaries visiting African countries are rarely taken to these poor spots, rather, they are flown in presidential planes or driven in limousines via routes that do not make them have the slightest clue of what is happening on the ground. Such is the smartness of our politicians, they make a show for an 'All is well' record. This had been aimed to conceal our misgivings from world attention. While this started as a game to present a good image to visitors, our own parliamentarians have taken two or more leaves from this presidential gimmick and have gone wild applying the same trick to the presidium each time they have visits to their constituencies. This would never have the poor man's plight addressed. We remain poor because no one was ever allowed to see our need!

We need to mention that poverty is not a self-made scenario but rather a design by those in power. The laws made are not supportive of new initiatives, and funds are never made available to seed the projects initiated by the have-nots. Poverty is a condition, not a curse! It is the absence of tools of production. In most African states, those who wield power own the former masters' business enterprises gotten through grabs, buy-ups, mergers, franchising and so on. This made the rich, richer. Because of mismanagement, the companies fall and close, living many people unemployed.

Poverty is exposed through many ways. Many people find themselves with nothing to do. They are not empowered at all. They lack the means to bring a meaningful life. Poverty breaks the brains of the bearer. It binds people from happiness. It kills one's ego, shatters the veins and sinks the soul. The problematic of poverty rests with the dictum that the poor has no say. Because they have nothing to say, they do not even say, even if they say, they are not listened to as they do not have an interest to protect. It creates an inferiority complex which continues to disempower the already poor and make them poorer. The poor assemble on their own to deliberate on how long their plight will last, but rarely do they talk of how they can uplift themselves because they have no means. Eventually, they encourage themselves to be resilient and soldier on till a divine intervention avails itself. Such is the institutionalization of poverty in African societies. The scenario is that the poor do not need large amounts of money, they just wish they had enough to eat, a roof over their heads, and clothes to put on. It is not about fat bank accounts, but a sustainable livelihood that revolves round making people manage their lives without welfare handouts.

We implore the governments to put laws that protect the people. There is need to promulgate investor friendly legislation to ensure the ease of doing business is enhanced. Small and Medium Enterprise development initiatives should be supported by investor friendly laws that are deliberately crafted to promote enterprise growth. Policies on profit commutation should not scare away foreign direct investment. National budgets should consider funding small sector investments, and offer seed capital avenues to alleviate penury. Most African states enjoy rich soils and average rainfall patterns, making agricultural projects viable. Governments should support farming by making inputs and implements available to poor farmers. Markets should be open to small holder farmers. Farming infrastructure should be constructed in the form of small dams, irrigation development initiatives and agricultural support services in order to convert our dry lands into greenbelts. Pricing policies should be competitive to allow affordability and product distribution. College students should be clustered to form companies and be availed funds to start businesses and create employment. Large conglomerates should create shareholding synergies that involve locals, and should be motivated into franchising indigenous peoples. Evidently, all people holding political posts should not be allowed to intervene in economics because once allowed, they would put in place laws that protect their interests instead of advancing commerce. It may also pay dividends to alert all governments to ensure there is a direct separation of politics from economics and allow the later to dance to market trends without interference. Governments should also reduce dependence on domestic borrowing to make funds available for enterprise development. A reduction on recurrent expenditure could be achieved through a deliberate streamlining of executive appointments. International missions should be limited to those destinations that have a direct bearing on management of bilateral commitments. Poverty in African nations is mainly a result of ballooned governments whose ministries duplicate each other, hence create fertile ground for bloated accountability, high levels of corruption and nepotistic appointments.

Lastly, the poor people should also take it upon themselves to emancipate themselves from the bondage of penury by way of cooperative ventures, whereby they pool resources and skills together in order to gain from the power of unity and the diversity of many over one. It has to be hopeful to accept that even in poverty, we are the mighty seed of our own success.

.

ABOUT THE AUTHORS

Ruxton Mudhabuko was born 1980, at Checheche, in Chipinge, Zimbabwe. He holds Diplomas in Philosophy and Religious Studies from the University of Zimbabwe's affiliate colleges. He is a Secondary school teacher in Buhera District, Zimbabwe. He believes that the constancy of change brings about cherished developments upon the face of the earth. This is his first publication.

Justice E T Mukuchura, the editor/publisher was born in Mutare, Zimbabwe. He holds a Certificate In Education (U.Z), Diploma in Journalism and Professional Writing(Transworld Tutorial College, U.K), and B.Tech in Education Management (Tech. Pretoria). He is a Primary school head teacher. He has published five poetry anthologies before his hand on this book. He believes in African Renaissance and Unity; The African Brotherhood.